CANTERBURY

A MISCELLANY

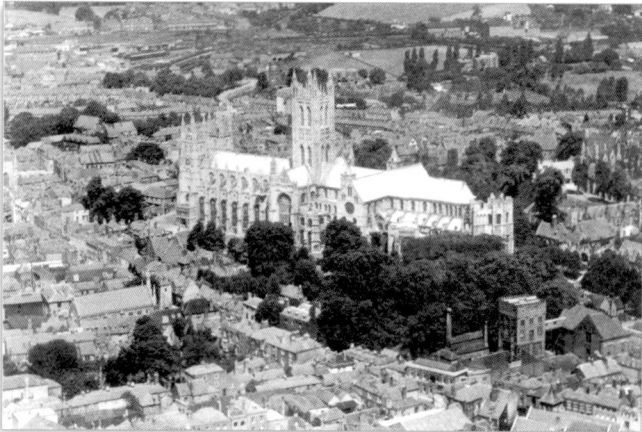

Compiled by Julia Skinner

With particular reference to the work of Martin Andrew

THE FRANCIS FRITH COLLECTION

www.francisfrith.com

First published in the United Kingdom in 2006 by The Francis Frith Collection®

This edition published exclusively for Oakridge Books & Gifts in 2010 ISBN 978-1-84589-549-5
Oakridge, Greenstalls Park, Costello Hill, Ilchester, Somerset BA22 8LB. Tel: 08453 893293

British Library Cataloguing in Publication Data

Did You Know? Canterbury - A Miscellany
Compiled by Julia Skinner
With particular reference to the work of Martin Andrew

The Francis Frith Collection
Frith's Barn, Teffont,
Salisbury, Wiltshire SP3 5QP
Tel: +44 (0) 1722 716 376
Email: info@francisfrith.co.uk
www.francisfrith.com

Printed and bound in England

Front Cover: **CANTERBURY, MERCERY LANE c1952** C18027p

The colour-tinting is for illustrative purposes only, and is not intended to be historically accurate

CONTENTS

INTRODUCTION

'Scarce any City is there in this Kingdom, which for antiquity of origins, or for the dignity of its fortune, can be compared with ours.' (John Twyne, Mayor of Canterbury, 1553-54)

Canterbury is famous the world over for its cathedral. The present building was founded by the Normans in 1070, but the nave was rebuilt to the designs of Henry Yevele between 1378 and 1405 and the central tower, Bell Harry Tower, was added c1500. The earliest Norman work is found in the crypt, the largest Norman crypt in Britain. Canterbury Cathedral has been an object of pilgrimage for many centuries, a pilgrimage immortalised by Geoffrey Chaucer (1335-1400) in his 'Canterbury Tales', which depicts a group of pilgrims setting out from Southwark to Canterbury. The object of their journey was the shrine of St Thomas Becket, the Archbishop of Canterbury famously martyred in 1170 by four of Henry II's over-zealous knights. Thomas Becket was canonised in 1173, and the shrine of St Thomas rapidly became the destination of one of the three major European pilgrimages; the other two were to Santiago de Compostela in western Spain and to Rome, the mother church in the Middle Ages of all Christendom.

'And specially, from every shires ende
Of Engelond, to Caunturbury they wende,
The hooly blisful martir for the seke
That hem hath holpen, whan that they were seeke ..'

Canterbury was heavily bombed by the Luftwaffe in 1942 during the 'Baedeker raids' of the Second World War; these were air raids deliberately aimed at some of the most historic British cities, chosen from the Baedeker guide books, and were an attempt by the Germans to lower British morale. The cathedral suffered some damage, but the bombs destroyed a great deal of the city itself. However, one result of the damage was that much evidence of Canterbury's Roman foundations was discovered during reconstruction work, and a great deal more is now known about the city's earliest years.

Despite the damage suffered both by war and modern development, Canterbury still contains many ancient buildings. Nowadays the pilgrims to the city take the form of modern tourists, who flock here in their thousands each year to soak up the atmosphere of this holy and historic place. The story of Canterbury is full of fascinating characters and events, of which this book can only provide a brief glimpse.

THE CATHEDRAL, THE NORMAN CRYPT 1888 21396

KENT DIALECT WORDS AND PHRASES

'Adam's ale' - water.

'Bread and cheese' - hawthorn leaves, which can be eaten and are supposed to taste of bread and cheese.

'Chimleys' - chimneys.

'Crawlybob' - a woodlouse.

'Flittermouse' - a bat.

'Howsomever' - however.

'Huffkin' - a type of soft bread roll.

'Pinchywig' - an earwig.

'Pom' - jam.

'Strig' - the stalk of a flower or fruit.

'Wirretin' - worrying or fussing over something.

It has been claimed that the term **'to canter'** may have originated from medieval pilgrims to Canterbury spurring their horses on to the faster 'Canterbury pace' of a gentle gallop as evening drew near, so that they could reach the city before its gates were shut for the night.

HAUNTED CANTERBURY

A surviving tower of Canterbury's medieval city walls at Pound Lane is called the Sudbury Tower, after Archbishop Simon of Sudbury who funded the rebuilding of part of the city defences in the 14th century. A bedroom in the tower is said to be haunted by a mysterious bearded man dressed in a grey robe, which some people think is the ghost of the archbishop himself.

The Marlowe Theatre, like many theatres across the country, is said to have a resident ghost, which can sometimes be seen watching the performances from the side of the stage.

The historic Weavers' House in the High Street is said to be haunted by a ghostly lady dressed in grey, who has been seen gliding up the staircase.

The cathedral is believed by some people to be haunted by a ghostly monk who walks the cloisters; those who have reported seeing the spectre before it suddenly vanishes have also noticed a sudden drop in temperature.

One of Canterbury's most famous ghost stories is that of the ghost of Nell Cook, who is said to haunt the Dark Entry in the cathedral precincts. Nell worked as a cook for a canon of the cathedral, and discovered that he was having an affair with a lady who had come to stay with him, supposedly his niece; Nell appears to have had unreciprocated feelings for the canon herself, and in a fit of jealousy murdered the canon and his lover by serving them with a poisoned pear pie. The cathedral authorities managed to keep the scandal quiet by quickly burying the bodies, but Nell herself disappeared soon after. Many years later, workmen in the Dark Entry found the skeleton of a woman, believed to be Nell's, in a pit beneath one of the flagstones of the passage; presumably she had been murdered herself, to keep her quiet, and her vengeful spirit is supposed to have roamed the area ever since. This ghost story featured in the 'Ingoldsby Legends' by R H Barham (1788-1845), who may well have invented the whole tale; Barham said that the ghost visited the passage on Friday nights, and that anyone who sees the apparition will be dead within the year.

CANTERBURY MISCELLANY

Before the Roman conquest of Britain of AD43, there was a prosperous Iron Age trading town named Durwhern in the Canterbury area, where trackways converged to cross the River Stour as it cut through the Downs. The Romans renamed the town Cantiacorum Durovernum, a Romanised version of Durwhern; the other element referred to the Cantiaci, the tribe of Kent. After the end of Roman rule, the whole of Kent fell to Germanic invaders from the North Sea coast and Denmark. A kingdom of Kent emerged, with Cantwarabyrig, meaning 'the burg, or defended settlement, of the Kentish people', as its capital.

Canterbury's Roman Museum has been built around the remains of a Roman town house which was discovered beneath the Longmarket shopping development (the entrance is in Butchery Lane). The house had several rooms and corridors with colourful mosaic floors, and some of these can be seen in the museum.

RUINED ARCHES OF THE INFIRMARY c1870 5292

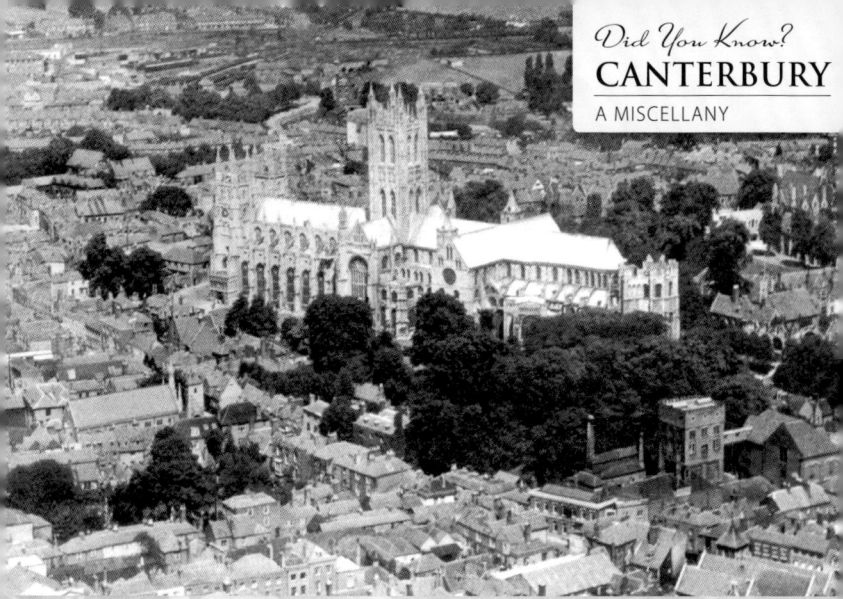

THE CATHEDRAL FROM THE AIR c1935 C18061

Photograph C18061, above, was taken before the Second World War, and shows the mighty cathedral towering above its surroundings, a walled city with narrow streets of two- and three-storey houses and shops, many of them medieval and Tudor in origin. In June 1942 all this changed with the devastating Baedeker air raids, when high explosive and incendiary bombs caused spectacular destruction to the city, although the cathedral itself escaped fairly lightly. Most of the buildings in the foreground of this photograph lay inside the city walls and were destroyed, exposing part of the city wall near the bus station.

During an archaeological excavation near Stour Street in the 1980s, the skeletons of a Romano-British family were found. The family of four appeared to have been brutally murdered and hastily buried, but the reason why will never be known.

In the Roman Museum in the Longmarket are two Roman cavalry swords which were found by workmen digging up a road near the old gasworks in the 1970s. They are extremely rare, as very few examples of cavalry swords have been found in Britain.

Beneath Watling Street and St Margaret's Street are the remains of Cantiacorum Durovernum's Roman theatre. In its final development it could seat 3,000 people, making it one of the largest theatres of Roman Britain. A section of the theatre can be seen in the cellar of a former hotel in St Margaret's Street.

THE CATHEDRAL c1875 12053

ST MARTIN'S CHURCH, QUEEN BERTHA'S TOMB 1898 40851

In the late 6th century Pope Gregory sent a mission to England to convert the Anglo-Saxon people to Christianity. The mission was led by Augustine (later St Augustine). He and his companions landed in south-east England and made for Canterbury, from where King Ethelbert ruled the kingdom of Kent. Ethelbert's wife Bertha, a Frankish princess, was already a practising Christian and worshipped in St Martin's Church, which probably dates back to a Christian church here that was founded during the Roman period. Ethelbert was baptised on Whitsunday, AD597. He allowed Augustine to found two monasteries, one outside the city walls, originally dedicated to St Peter and St Paul but which later became known as St Augustine's Abbey, and Christ Church Priory within the walls. Augustine and most of the Anglo-Saxon archbishops and Kentish kings were buried in St Augustine's Abbey, while Christ Church Priory became the archbishop's seat, or 'cathedra'.

DANE JOHN GARDENS 1921 70333

The first castle in Canterbury was a wooden 'motte and bailey' castle at Dane John. In the late 18th century the Dane John Mound was created to mark the spot, surrounded by an attractive park. The early castle was replaced by Canterbury Castle, which was completed during the reign of Henry I (1100-1135). This was one of the first castles in England to be built of stone, but its ruined keep off Castle Street, once one of the largest in the country, is all that remains.

During the Roman period, the town of Cantiacorum Durovernum was very important, for here the Roman road now called Watling Street passed on its way from the port of Richborough (the gateway to Britannia) to London and beyond. Roads from two other Roman ports also converged here, one from Dover and the other from Lympne. There were also roads to Reculver and to the port at Fordwich on the River Stour. The town thrived, complete with baths, a forum, an amphitheatre and defensive walls.

St Martin's Church, which is believed to date from the Roman period, was where Augustine and his monks based themselves soon after arriving in Canterbury in AD597, making it the oldest parish church in England where Christian worship has taken place continuously. The tomb seen in photograph 40851, on page 9, is traditionally known as Queen Bertha's Tomb, but it is now believed that the queen's remains were later moved from this church to the monastery church of St Peter and St Paul, which eventually became St Augustine's Abbey, to lie next to her husband, King Ethelbert.

Long stretches (about 1 mile) of Canterbury's Norman and medieval city walls, built on Roman foundations, are still visible - the best sections can be seen at Dane John and Broad Street. A small fragment of the Roman Queningate can still be seen opposite the Great Gate of St Augustine's Abbey, and foundations of the Roman wall can be seen at Burgate and Northgate (where a huge length is built into the Church of St Mary there). The medieval walls once included 21 watch-towers, many of which have survived, although they have often been incorporated into houses.

**THE CATHEDRAL,
THE ENTRANCE TO THE TRINITY CHAPEL 1890** 25690

After the Norman Conquest of 1066, King William's half-brother Odo, Bishop of Bayeux, was made Earl of Kent. It was Bishop Odo who commissioned the Bayeux Tapestry (actually an embroidery) to depict the events of the conquest, probably to display at the dedication of his new cathedral in Bayeux in 1077. Stylistic and textual analysis of the Bayeux Tapestry has led many scholars to believe that it was made in Canterbury, where there was a famous school at the time which was renowned all over western Europe for producing large-scale needleworks depicting narratives in pictorial form. The work, which appears to have been made in 'the Canterbury tradition', was probably designed by one person, and created by a group of nuns who were highly skilled in such work.

Canterbury's Anglo-Saxon cathedral burnt down in 1067, the year after the Norman Conquest. According to Eadmer, a Christ Church monk who was a boy at the time of the fire, 'the city of Canterbury was set on fire by the carelessness of some persons, and the rising flames caught the mother church thereof and the whole was consumed', but it is now believed that the Normans burnt down the cathedral deliberately to leave a clear space for a new building. King William replaced the Anglo-Saxon Archbishop Stigand with Lanfranc, the abbot of his royal abbey at Caen in Normandy. Eadmer says that when Lanfranc 'came to Canterbury and found that the church of the Saviour, which he had undertaken to rule, was reduced to almost nothing by fire and ruin, he was filled with consternation. He pulled down to the ground all that he found of the burnt monastery, whether of buildings or the wasted remains of buildings, and having dug out their foundations from under the earth, he built in their stead others which greatly excelled them both in beauty and size. As for the church, which the said fire, combined with age, has rendered completely unserviceable, he set about to destroy utterly and erect a more noble one.' This building work was achieved by 1077, in astonishingly quick time. Lanfranc's work still survives to some extent. The north transept and part of the south remain in recognisable form: his crossing tower piers are encased in the 15th-century piers, while the lower part of the north nave remains.

The cathedral assumed its architectural greatness in the early 12th century. Under Lanfranc's successor Archbishop Anselm, later St Anselm, Prior Ernulf and then Prior Conrad rebuilt the east arm of the cathedral on a stupendous scale following a collapse, probably of part of Lanfranc's choir. William of Malmesbury recorded that 'Ernulf … rebuilt the fallen chief part of the church which Lanfranc had erected so magnificently that nothing of the kind could be seen in England for its blaze of glass windows, for its glitter of marble paving, and its painting of many hues'. William was describing what is now known as 'the Glorious Choir' which Prior Conrad 'magnificently completed … and when finished he adorned it with noteworthy painting, and so adorned he enriched it with precious ornaments'. This choir was dedicated in 1130. Unfortunately it was built with a timber roof which was destroyed by fire in 1174, but it was rebuilt in glorious style - see photograph 70340 on page 19.

The early view of the cathedral shown in photograph 6199, opposite, shows how at ground level the nave is dominated by the deep buttresses that carry the thrust of the nave vaults to the ground. In the case of the west towers, the buttresses are so deep by the time they reach the ground that they enclose the porches and provide surfaces big enough for rows of statues in niches. The rows of holes seen in this photograph above porch level are 'put-log' holes into which the timber scaffolding poles were inserted during the building of the cathedral. They have now been plugged with stone.

In 1170 a cataclysmic event shook the whole of western Christendom: the dispute between the stubborn Archbishop of Canterbury, Thomas Becket, and Henry II boiled over, and the archbishop was brutally murdered in the north transept of the cathedral by four knights. The knights had over-zealously interpreted the king's angry outburst 'Will no one rid me of this turbulent priest!', and seeking to ingratiate themselves with the king they hurried to Canterbury, where they attacked and killed Becket, cleaving his skull with their swords. Henry II was appalled by Becket's murder and underwent many penances, including flogging by the Canterbury monks.

THE CATHEDRAL, THE SOUTH-WEST CORNER c1872 6199

After another major fire in the cathedral in 1174, the choir was rebuilt spectacularly (see photograph 70340, opposite). Canterbury had become the premier place of pilgrimage since the martyrdom of Archbishop Thomas Becket in 1170; the pilgrims needed an awe-inspiring experience, and the monks gave them one. The new choir was designed by William of Sens, a French master mason who was skilled in the Gothic style of northern France, with its pointed arches and universal stone-built ribbed vaults. Canterbury's immense prestige meant that the style chosen became the English norm; it sounded the final death knell of the already declining Anglo-Norman style. William of Sens fell from the scaffolding during construction, and the work was completed by another William, 'the Englishman'. Construction began in 1175 and was finished in 1184.

Gervase of Canterbury wrote an invaluable account of the rebuilding work in the cathedral in the late 12th century, and described how in 1179 William of Sens 'was in the act of preparing machines for the turning of the great (choir) vault, when suddenly the beams broke beneath his feet and he fell to the ground, stones and timber accompanying his fall, from the height of the capitals of the upper vault, that is to say fifty feet. The master, thus hurt, remained in his bed for some time … and perceiving that he gained no benefit from the physicians, gave up the work and returned to his home in France. And another succeeded him in charge of the works: William by name, English by nation, small in body, but in workmanship of many kinds acute and honest'. William the Englishman was responsible for the design of the Trinity Choir, which housed the shrine of St Thomas, and the Corona, so named because this was where St Thomas's crown was kept, the top of his skull, which was severed by the swords of his murderers.

THE CATHEDRAL, THE CHOIR, LOOKING EAST 1921 70340

**THE CATHEDRAL,
BELL HARRY TOWER 1888** 21359

Photograph 25690, on page 14, shows the entrance into the Trinity Chapel, which housed the shrine of St Thomas. The view shows how much higher the floor of the chapel is than the western part of the choir, which is itself raised on the crypt. This raising may have been quite deliberate, to emphasise the hierarchy of the building and the importance of Thomas Becket's shrine.

The sublime crossing tower of Canterbury Cathedral now known as the Bell Harry Tower was completed by the beginning of the 16th century (see photograph 21359, opposite). Formerly known as the Angel Steeple because of the gilded angel figure topping the old, low Norman central tower, the new tower was designed by John Wastell, the King's Master Mason, who worked on it from the mid 15th century to 1503. The tower soars to 235ft, and was built in two stages. The tower's surface is richly carved, and the walls are framed by heavily-modelled soaring angel turrets; it is perhaps the finest crossing tower of medieval England. The lower stage, the lantern, has its windows open to the crossing far below, and has the most wonderful fan vault. The tower is built of brick and faced with stone. Bell Harry sits in a frame on top of the tower.

> Buried at the rear of the Warriors' (St Michael's) Chapel of the cathedral is Archbishop Stephan Langton, who presided over the sealing of the Magna Carta by King John in 1215.

Adjoining the cathedral was once the Benedictine monastery of Christ Church Priory. Nearby, around Green Court, parts of the monastery are incorporated in the buildings of King's School, one of the oldest of English public schools. Former old boys of King's School include the Elizabethan playwright Christopher Marlowe, William Harvey (the scientist who discovered the circulation of the blood), the novelist William Somerset Maugham, and the astronaut Michael Foale, the first Briton to perform a space walk.

Photograph 25689x, opposite, shows the monument in the cathedral to Canon Alexander Chapman, who died in 1629. The carving is attributed to Nicholas Stone. At the time this photograph was taken the monument was in the north transept, where Thomas Becket was murdered; it has now been moved to the choir aisle, and in its place in the north transept is a modern sculpture of bronze swords, symbolising the martyrdom of Becket.

The round-topped rendered brick tomb chest in the Trinity Chapel of Canterbury Cathedral, shown in photograph 1085, opposite, is that of the exiled French Cardinal de Chatillon, Odo Coligny, who was murdered by a treacherous servant who is said to have given him a poisoned apple. Although a cardinal, he had Huguenot leanings; he was given asylum by Elizabeth I in 1568, having fled from France, which was then in the grip of the Wars of Religion.

The massive twin-towered West Gate (see photograph C18047, opposite) is the only survivor of the medieval gates which once interrupted the path of the Norman wall around the city - all but West Gate were pulled down in the 1780s. West Gate was rebuilt c 1380 for Archbishop Simon of Sudbury. Until 1829 it was the city jail, but in 1906 it became a museum of arms and armour.

The cathedral is famous for its medieval stained-glass, one of the oldest collections in the country. The Miracle Windows in the cathedral illustrate the life and death of St Thomas Becket. Other windows known as the Poor Man's Bible depict scenes from the Old and New Testaments for the illiterate.

**THE CATHEDRAL,
THE CHAPMAN MONUMENT
1890** 25689x

**THE CATHEDRAL,
THE TRINITY CHAPEL c1862** 1085

WEST GATE AND ST DUNSTAN'S STREET c1955 C18047

GREYFRIARS 1924 76111

Photograph 76111, above, shows what was probably the dormitory of Canterbury's once great Franciscan friary, the Greyfriars, which was established c1267, hidden behind Greyfriars House in Stour Street. The building spans a branch of the River Stour with a twin arch, the central pier in the river bed, and is the oldest Franciscan building in Britain. It is no longer accessible by the path along the river bank, and the best view of its restored elevations is from the nearby bridge over the river. The upper floor of Greyfriars is now used as a chapel for weekly worship.

Photograph C18041, below, shows the view from inside the city walls through the arch of West Gate to St Dunstan's Street. The route through this gate was taken by Henry II when he came to Canterbury as a penitent in 1174, after the murder of Thomas Becket in 1170, and by Henry V on his triumphant return from France and the victory of the Battle of Agincourt in 1415.

ST PETER'S STREET c1955 C18041

Leading to the cathedral, the narrow alleyway of Mercery Lane with its overhanging shops was the usual route by which pilgrims approached the climax of their journey (see photograph C18027, opposite). In medieval times it would have been lined with shops and stalls selling religious medallions, phials of water from Becket's Well in the cathedral crypt and other memorabilia. Behind the later facades are many medieval timber-framed buildings; those on the left were built as part of the Chequers of Hope Inn for pilgrims in the 1390s. It was built around a vast square. The second floor was a 100-bed dormitory, and the first floor was individual chambers. Most of the left-hand buildings are now part of the Debenhams store.

Congregational numbers at the cathedral nowadays can vary. There are two services a day, and three on Sundays, and at the 11am eucharist on a Sunday between 250-300 worshippers can pour through the south porch. However, for most services each day the congregation is between 30-40. Today, Canterbury Cathedral costs £9,000 per day to keep open and in good repair. Apart from its main religious purpose, it also attracts over one million visitors each year.

From the late 16th century a number of Huguenots and Walloons fled from religious persecution in France and Flanders and came to England, bringing with them their weaving skills, especially of silk. Some of them came to Canterbury, and the Weavers' House in the High Street (now a restaurant) was the centre of much of their industry (see photograph 70331a, opposite). It once housed hundreds of looms and the river below was used in part of the cloth-making process. Some of these Huguenot refugees prospered, they contributed a great deal to Canterbury, and some of them became councillors, including Alderman Sabine, who is believed to have built the timber-fronted 'leaning house' at 28 Palace Street, once known as the King's School Shop; Avery Sabine was a woolcomber and his initials are near the door. Historians believe that the house was built by Sabine to house weavers; the small windows at the bottom of the building were to let in the light as the weavers worked. The house is famous because it appears to be resting on the building next door, and its front door is sharply angled.

MERCERY LANE c1952 C18027

THE WEAVERS' HOUSE 1921 70331a

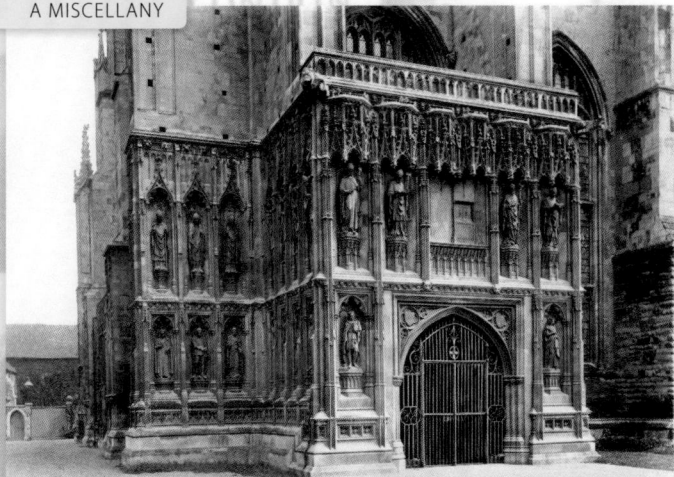

THE CATHEDRAL, THE SOUTH PORCH 1890 25680

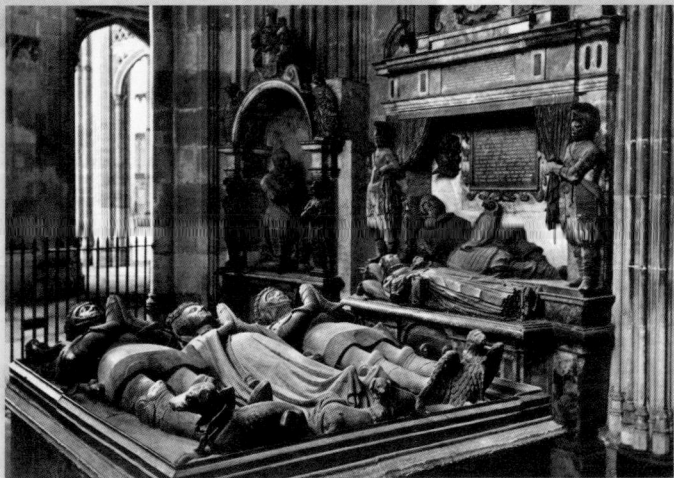

THE CATHEDRAL, TOMBS IN THE WARRIORS' CHAPEL c1862 1087

The South Porch was entirely refaced in 1862, and new statues were added. The doorway is flanked by Ethelbert, King of Kent, whom St Augustine converted to Christianity in AD597, and his queen, Bertha. Above are Augustine, Lanfranc, Anselm and Thomas Cranmer, who were all important Archbishops of Canterbury.

St Michael's Chapel in the cathedral, also known as the Warriors' Chapel, was built for Lady Margaret Holland, daughter of the Earl of Kent, who died a few days after the chapel was dedicated in May 1439. In pride of place in the centre of the chapel is the tomb chest of Lady Margaret, shown in photograph 1087, opposite. She lies between her two coroneted husbands, John Beaufort, Earl of Somerset and son of John of Gaunt, and Thomas, Duke of Clarence, the second son of Henry IV. She married well, and both husbands predeceased her.

The Warriors' (St Michael's) Chapel of the cathedral is now the Chapel of the Royal East Kent Regiment, the Buffs, and is hung with their battle flags. Although the regiment no longer exists, due to cutbacks and amalgamations, the chapel holds its Book of Remembrance, listing its officers and men who fell in both World Wars; each day at 11am the bell of HMS 'Canterbury' outside the chapel is struck, and a representative from the local regiment at the Howe barracks turns a page of the book, 'lest we forget'.

Photograph 21389, opposite, shows the north walk of the Great Cloister, in poor repair at the time of this view, but now restored. This walk contained the monks' lavatorium, the two open bays on the left of the photograph, which was where the monks washed their hands before meals. Its canopy has been partially reinstated in the recent restoration.

Behind iron railings in photograph 21379 (opposite) lies the gilded bronze effigy of Edward the Black Prince, the victor over the French at the Battles of Crécy and Poitiers, who predeceased his father, Edward III, in 1376. Above is a wooden tester canopy with a contemporary painting showing God and his crucified Son; above that are suspended replicas of the prince's armour - the originals are now in a glass case in the south choir aisle. The chantry chapel for the prince and his wife, Joan, the Fair Maid of Kent, is in the crypt, and is now the French Protestant Church.

The only King of England buried in the cathedral was Henry IV, together with his queen, Joan of Navarre (see photograph 21380, opposite). Their tomb is splendid and ornate, and the alabaster effigies are both portraits: this was confirmed when the tomb was opened in 1832, and the bodies were found to be perfectly preserved, with the king's beard still thick and russet in colour.

THE CLOISTERS, THE LAVATORIUM 1888 21389

**THE CATHEDRAL, THE TOMB OF
THE BLACK PRINCE 1888** 21379

**THE CATHEDRAL, THE TOMB OF
HENRY IV 1888** 21380

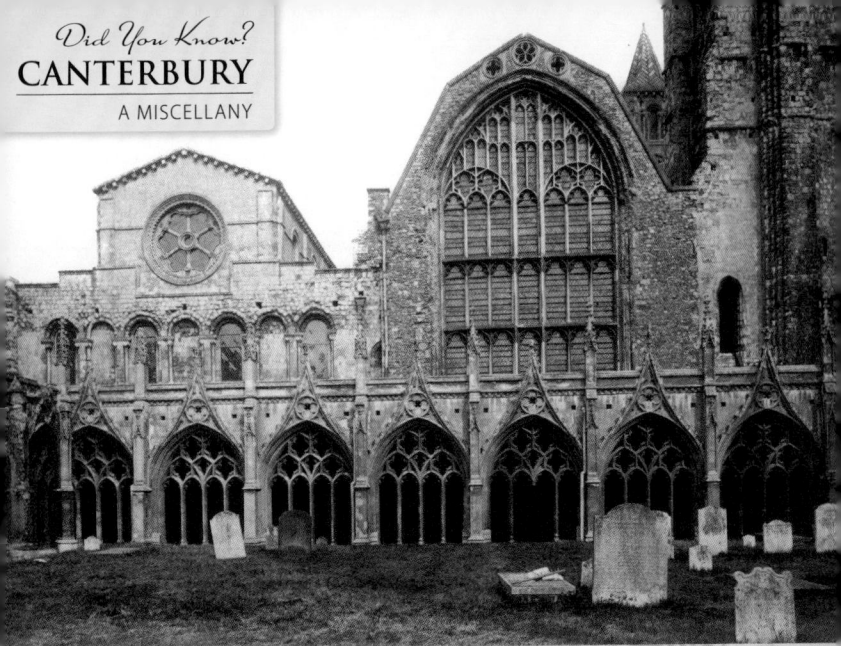

THE CLOISTERS 1888 21361

Beyond the cathedral lay the Benedictine priory of Christ Church, the Anglo-Saxon priory greatly enlarged by Lanfranc; a remarkable amount of Norman work survives, both Lanfranc's and 12th-century. Photograph 21361, above, was taken looking east: the tall buttress of Lanfranc's north transept is on the right, then the huge west window of the Chapter House, rebuilt in 1304. To the left is the Norman Great Dorter, or monks' dormitory, and the wheel window belongs to the neo-Norman library of 1867, which was destroyed by bombs in the Second World War. The library was rebuilt in the 1950s in a conservative style with Tudor flint and stone upper floors over a Norman arched passageway to recreate the cloister's west side.

To the right of the gatehouse of the cathedral, seen in photograph 70336, below, was the monks' necessarium, or reredorter, both of which were medieval euphemisms for the monastic lavatories or privies. The present view into the infirmary cloister was then not possible, as the lavatories closed off the monks' world from Green Court. There were 56 privy seats provided, and they were flushed by water from the water tower.

THE CATHEDRAL, THE NORTH SIDE 1921 70336

THE MUSEUM OF CANTERBURY
2005 C18704

The Museum of Canterbury in Stour Street (see photograph C18704, opposite) is housed in one of Canterbury's finest medieval buildings, in what was formerly the Poor Priests' Hospital ('hospital' in those days meant accommodation, or a 'hostel'). The building was at one time also used as a workhouse for the destitute. Amongst the fascinating exhibits in the museum is a collection of medieval pilgrim badges. These badges were usually made of pewter, and were bought by pilgrims in the Middle Ages to show all the places that had been visited, in much the same way as some people nowadays collect souvenir badges from tourist spots. The Canterbury badges usually bore a likeness of St Thomas.

In the Museum of Canterbury is a fine account of the day in 1620 when a Canterbury grocer, Robert Cushman, led negotiations at an inn in Palace Street to hire a ship, the 'Mayflower', to transport the religious and political dissenters known as the Pilgrim Fathers to America. Cushman himself sailed in a second ship, the 'Speedwell', and arrived in the New World in 1621. However he returned to Canterbury, where he died in 1625, although his son, Thomas, became a ruling elder of the congregation at the Plymouth settlement in Massachusetts. One of the Cushmans' descendants was General Robert E Lee.

In the Museum of Canterbury is the 'Invicta' engine that was built by Robert Stephenson for what became known as the Crab and Winkle Line, the world's first passenger railway. In May 1830 passengers paid 9d for a 40-minute trip from Canterbury to Whitstable on a train pulled by this engine. It went at about nine miles an hour after leaving its stop at North Lane in Canterbury. The engine itself was unable to climb up any sort of incline along the route, so great winches were installed at the top of the hills to wind it up the track.

A VIEW OF THE WEAVERS' HOUSE c1955 C18063

The Elizabethan playwright Christopher Marlowe was born in Canterbury, probably in 1564, and educated at King's School; his father, John, was a cobbler in the city. Marlowe is best known for his plays 'Tamburlaine the Great', 'Edward II' and 'The Tragical History of Dr Faustus', and his poetry, one of the most popular works being 'The Passionate Shepherd to his Love'. The Marlowe Theatre in Canterbury is named after him. The Marlowe family had a reputation for being loud, boisterous and often at war with its neighbours. One of Christopher's sisters was known for being a 'scowld', but it is not known whether she was ever subjected to the humiliation of Canterbury's ducking stool over the River Stour near the Weavers' House. The ducking stool seen in the foreground of photograph C18063, above, is a modern replica of the stool used in medieval times to punish nagging women by ducking them in the river. It was also used to test women suspected of being witches by submerging them in the river - if they were guilty they would survive by using their magic powers, but if they were innocent they would drown.

To the left of photograph 21402, below, is Court Gate, the main gateway into Christ Church Priory for visitors, travellers, pilgrims and the needy. This high Norman archway of the 1150s was infilled with lower Perpendicular Gothic arches by Prior Chillenden c1400; he also added the upper storey. To the right of the photograph are three bays of the heavily-restored Aula Nova, or new hall, which was originally over 150ft and nine bays long. The Aula Nova was built as a dormitory and refectory for poor pilgrims and visitors. It was raised over an undercroft, three surviving arches of which are seen here. The upper floor was largely rebuilt in the 19th century, but the covered stairway to the upper floor hall, seen on the right of the photograph, is one of the most remarkable survivals of the Norman cathedral priory. It dates from the 1150s.

THE NORMAN STAIR 1888 21402

**THE HOSPITAL OF ST THOMAS THE MARTYR
(THE EASTBRIDGE HOSPITAL) 2005** C18709

In medieval times poor pilgrims to the shrine of St Thomas rested at the Hospital of St Thomas the Martyr, later known as the Eastbridge Hospital. After the destruction of the shrine of St Thomas Becket in 1538, when Henry VIII ordered it to be stripped of its treasures and destroyed, the hospital was converted into almshouses for ten poor people of the city. Nowadays the Eastbridge Hospital is open to visitors on most days (see photograph C18709, above).

What are believed to be parts of the original stone pillars which once supported the shrine of St Thomas Becket are now on show in the Museum of Canterbury. The pieces were discovered in the River Stour and were recovered by divers; they were presumably thrown in the river after Henry VIII's men ransacked and destroyed the tomb.

The House of Agnes (the Dickens Inn) in St Dunstan's Street was described by Charles Dickens in 'David Copperfield' as the home of Agnes Wickfield, the daughter of the solicitor (see photograph C18701, below).

THE HOUSE OF AGNES (THE DICKENS INN), ST DUNSTAN'S STREET 2005 C18701

Photograph 21407, below, shows Christchurch Gate, now the main entrance to the cathedral precincts for visitors. This view shows the great Tudor gateway of 1502-1521 in its unrestored, crumbling state. It was restored in 1937, regaining its tall outer turrets, by the Friends of Canterbury Cathedral. The central niche now holds a bronze statue, 'The Welcoming Christ', by Klaus Ringhals, which was added in 1990 to commemorate the Friends' diamond jubilee.

CHRISTCHURCH GATE 1888 21407

SPORTING CANTERBURY

The St Lawrence cricket ground is Canterbury's best-known sporting venue. It has been home to Kent County Cricket Club since the 19th century, and has hosted international cricket. However its most famous feature is a tree. For many years a large lime tree grew within the area of the playing surface, unique in English county cricket. Sadly, the tree blew down in early 2005, during winter gales. However the cricket club had planned for such an event, and had already begun growing a replacement, which was planted by the legendary cricketer Colin Cowdrey.

The St Lawrence ground is not the only ground in the city to have been home to first-class cricket. The Beverley Ground was the venue for a number of matches from 1841-1846. The games included Kent v England, and Kent v The Gentlemen of England.

Only four men have scored 100 and taken 10 wickets in the same innings of a first-class cricket match, and one of them achieved this feat at Canterbury. EM Grace, brother of the famous WG Grace, was the successful player, playing for the MCC against The Gentlemen of Kent in 1862.

Canterbury City FC holds the dubious record of having one of the smallest attendances ever recorded in the Southern Football League. Just 38 people attended their match against Weymouth during the 1993-94 season. It was a very poor season for the club, who were relegated to the Kent League at the end of the season. Sadly, the club disbanded in 2001.

Canterbury Rugby Club has enjoyed plenty of success in recent times. In 2005/6 they became the first east Kent club to reach the National Leagues, and in the same season won the Kent Cup for the third time, defeating the famous Blackheath in the final.

Four different sports have taken place at the Kingsmead Stadium. Opened in 1958, it was the home of Canterbury City FC, Kent Crusaders Speedway team, as well as a venue for athletics and greyhound racing.

QUIZ QUESTIONS

Answers on page 48.

1. Thomas Becket was not the only Archbishop of Canterbury to be murdered. Who were the other two?

2. Canterbury Cathedral is the last resting-place of Edward the Black Prince, eldest son of Edward III. Prince Edward's wife Joan was renowned for her great beauty, and was known as 'the Fair Maid of Kent'. What was unusual about their marriage?

3. What was the reason for the Plum Pudding Riots, which took place in Canterbury in 1647?

4. How did the Bell Harry Tower of the cathedral get its name?

5. Who wrote the play 'Murder in the Cathedral', a dramatisation of the murder of Thomas Becket?

6. The Canterbury-born artist T S Cooper (Sidney Cooper) is particularly famous for his paintings of … what?

7. Which famous cartoon bear was created by a Canterbury artist?

8. What is the link between Canterbury and the successful 'The Lord of the Rings' trilogy of films?

9. Canterbury is twinned with which city?

10. What relic of ancient Canterbury can be seen in the Waterstone's bookshop in St Margaret's Street?

THE CATHEDRAL, THE WEST TOWERS 1890 25679

RECIPE

CANTERBURY PUDDING

Ingredients

75g/3oz self-raising flour
75g/3oz fresh breadcrumbs
75g/3oz shredded suet
50g/2oz caster sugar

Zest and juice of 1 lemon
1 egg, beaten
3 tablespoonfuls brandy
3 tablespoonfuls milk

Preheat the oven to 180 degrees C/350 degrees F/Gas Mark 4.

Mix together the flour, breadcrumbs, suet and sugar, and stir in the lemon zest. Make a well in the centre and add the beaten egg, lemon juice, brandy and enough milk to give a soft dropping consistency. Pour into a greased 1.1litre/2 pint pudding dish, and bake, uncovered, for about 1 hour until well risen. Serve hot with custard or cream.

THE CATHEDRAL, THE VIEW FROM THE CORONA CRYPT 1890 25694

WEST GATE AND THE RIVER STOUR c1955 C18044

RECIPE

KENTISH CHERRY BATTER PUDDING

Ingredients

45ml/3 tablespoonfuls kirsch (optional)
450g/1lb dark cherries, pitted
50g/2oz plain flour

50g/2oz caster sugar
2 eggs, separated
300ml/½ pint milk
75g/3oz butter, melted

Sprinkle the kirsch, if used, over the cherries in a small bowl, and leave them to soak for about 30 minutes.

Mix the flour and sugar together, then slowly stir in the egg yolks and milk to make a smooth batter. Stir in half the melted butter, and leave for 30 minutes.

Preheat the oven to 220 degrees C/425 degrees F/Gas Mark 7. Pour the remaining butter into a 600ml/1 pint baking dish, and put in the oven to heat. Whisk the egg whites until stiff, then fold them into the batter with the cherries and kirsch, if used, and pour the mixture into the baking dish. Bake for about 15 minutes, then reduce the oven temperature to 180 degrees C/350 degrees F/Gas Mark 4 and bake for a further 20 minutes, until golden and set in the centre. Serve hot, sprinkled with sugar, with custard or cream.

QUIZ ANSWERS

1. St Aelfheah, also known as St Alphege, became Archbishop of Canterbury in 1005, and was captured by Danish raiders when they attacked the city in 1011. They took the archbishop to their base at Greenwich, where they pelted him to death with ox bones in fury at his refusal to allow the country to be burdened with the cost of raising a ransom for his release. Another archbishop, Simon of Sudbury, was beheaded by the rebels in 1381, during the Peasants' Revolt; his tomb can be seen on the left of photograph 25690 on page 14. Two other archbishops who met violent ends were Thomas Cranmer, burned at the stake during the reign of Queen Mary, and William Laud, who was beheaded during the reign of Charles I.

2. Apart from the fact that Edward and Joan were cousins, the marriage was known to be a love-match, which was so unusual in the Middle Ages that in some circles it was considered shocking!

3. The Plum Pudding Riots which took place in 1647 during the Civil War occurred after Christmas celebrations in Canterbury were banned by Puritan extremists. The streets of the city were filled with Royalist rioters, and people declared they were on the side of 'God, King Charles and Kent'. In retaliation, Oliver Cromwell ordered the sector of the city walls between the castle and the West Gate to be demolished.

4. Bell Harry Tower is named after the original bell which was given for the central tower of the cathedral in 1316 by Prior Henry (Harry) Eastry. The purpose of the original bell was to call, or summon, the congregation to services, and the bell in the tower still functions as a 'calling bell' today.

5. T S Eliot.

6. Sidney Cooper is famous for his pastoral scenes, particularly for his depictions of cattle. The Sidney Cooper Gallery in St Peter's Street was originally an art school which was founded by the artist in 1882. A special gallery at the Royal Museum and Art Gallery in Canterbury's High Street is devoted to Cooper's work.

7. Rupert Bear. He was created by Mary Tourtel, who was born in Canterbury in 1874 and studied at the Simon Langton School and the Sidney Cooper Art School. Rupert first appeared in the Daily Express in 1920, and is the subject of his own museum in the city, the Rupert Bear Museum in Stour Street.

8. The actor Orlando Bloom, who played the elf Legolas in the films, was born in Canterbury in 1977, and educated at St Edmund's School.

9. Canterbury is twinned with Reims in France.

10. Part of the hypocaust, or under-floor heating system, of the ancient bath complex of the Roman town of Cantiacorum Durovernum is on show on the basement floor of the Waterstone's bookshop in St Margaret's Street.

WESTGATE GARDENS c1955   C18018

Did You Know?
CANTERBURY
A MISCELLANY

FRANCIS FRITH

PIONEER VICTORIAN PHOTOGRAPHER

Francis Frith, founder of the world-famous photographic archive, was a complex and multi-talented man. A devout Quaker and a highly successful Victorian businessman, he was philosophical by nature and pioneering in outlook. By 1855 he had already established a wholesale grocery business in Liverpool, and sold it for the astonishing sum of £200,000, which is the equivalent today of over £15,000,000. Now in his thirties, and captivated by the new science of photography, Frith set out on a series of pioneering journeys up the Nile and to the Near East.

INTRIGUE AND EXPLORATION

He was the first photographer to venture beyond the sixth cataract of the Nile. Africa was still the mysterious 'Dark Continent', and Stanley and Livingstone's historic meeting was a decade into the future. The conditions for picture taking confound belief. He laboured for hours in his wicker dark-room in the sweltering heat of the desert, while the volatile chemicals fizzed dangerously in their trays. Back in London he exhibited his photographs and was 'rapturously cheered' by members of the Royal Society. His reputation as a photographer was made overnight.

VENTURE OF A LIFE-TIME

By the 1870s the railways had threaded their way across the country, and Bank Holidays and half-day Saturdays had been made obligatory by Act of Parliament. All of a sudden the working man and his family were able to enjoy days out, take holidays, and see a little more of the world.

With typical business acumen, Francis Frith foresaw that these new tourists would enjoy having souvenirs to commemorate their days out. For the next thirty years he travelled the country by train and by pony and trap, producing fine photographs of seaside resorts and beauty spots that were keenly bought by millions of Victorians. These prints were painstakingly pasted into family albums and pored over during the dark nights of winter, rekindling precious memories of summer excursions. Frith's studio was soon supplying retail shops all over the country, and by 1890 F Frith & Co had become the greatest specialist photographic publishing company in the world, with over 2,000 sales outlets, and pioneered the picture postcard.

FRANCIS FRITH'S LEGACY

Francis Frith had died in 1898 at his villa in Cannes, his great project still growing. By 1970 the archive he created contained over a third of a million pictures showing 7,000 British towns and villages.

Frith's legacy to us today is of immense significance and value, for the magnificent archive of evocative photographs he created provides a unique record of change in the cities, towns and villages throughout Britain over a century and more. Frith and his fellow studio photographers revisited locations many times down the years to update their views, compiling for us an enthralling and colourful pageant of British life and character.

We are fortunate that Frith was dedicated to recording the minutiae of everyday life. For it is this sheer wealth of visual data, the painstaking chronicle of changes in dress, transport, street layouts, buildings, housing and landscape that captivates us so much today, offering us a powerful link with the past and with the lives of our ancestors.

Computers have now made it possible for Frith's many thousands of images to be accessed almost instantly. The archive offers every one of us an opportunity to examine the places where we and our families have lived and worked down the years. Its images, depicting our shared past, are now bringing pleasure and enlightenment to millions around the world a century and more after his death.

For further information visit: www.francisfrith.com

INTERIOR DECORATION

Frith's photographs can be seen framed and as giant wall murals in thousands of pubs, restaurants, hotels, banks, retail stores and other public buildings throughout Britain. These provide interesting and attractive décor, generating strong local interest and acting as a powerful reminder of gentler days in our increasingly busy and frenetic world.

FRITH PRODUCTS

All Frith photographs are available as prints and posters in a variety of different sizes and styles. In the UK we also offer a range of other gift and stationery products illustrated with Frith photographs, although many of these are not available for delivery outside the UK – see our web site for more information on the products available for delivery in your country.

THE INTERNET

Over 100,000 photographs of Britain can be viewed and purchased on the Frith web site. The web site also includes memories and reminiscences contributed by our customers, who have personal knowledge of localities and of the people and properties depicted in Frith photographs. If you wish to learn more about a specific town or village you may find these reminiscences fascinating to browse. Why not add your own comments if you think they would be of interest to others? See **www.francisfrith.com**

PLEASE HELP US BRING FRITH'S PHOTOGRAPHS TO LIFE

Our authors do their best to recount the history of the places they write about. They give insights into how particular towns and villages developed, they describe the architecture of streets and buildings, and they discuss the lives of famous people who lived there. But however knowledgeable our authors are, the story they tell is necessarily incomplete.

Frith's photographs are so much more than plain historical documents. They are living proofs of the flow of human life down the generations. They show real people at real moments in history; and each of those people is the son or daughter of someone, the brother or sister, aunt or uncle, grandfather or grandmother of someone else. All of them lived, worked and played in the streets depicted in Frith's photographs.

We would be grateful if you would give us your insights into the places shown in our photographs: the streets and buildings, the shops, businesses and industries. Post your memories of life in those streets on the Frith website: what it was like growing up there, who ran the local shop and what shopping was like years ago; if your workplace is shown tell us about your working day and what the building is used for now. Read other visitors' memories and reconnect with your shared local history and heritage. With your help more and more Frith photographs can be brought to life, and vital memories preserved for posterity, and for the benefit of historians in the future.

Wherever possible, we will try to include some of your comments in future editions of our books. Moreover, if you spot errors in dates, titles or other facts, please let us know, because our archive records are not always completely accurate—they rely on 140 years of human endeavour and hand-compiled records. You can email us using the contact form on the website.

Thank you!

For further information, trade, or author enquiries
please contact us at the address below:

**The Francis Frith Collection, Frith's Barn, Teffont,
Salisbury, Wiltshire, England SP3 5QP.**
Tel: +44 (0)1722 716 376 Fax: +44 (0)1722 716 881
e-mail: sales@francisfrith.co.uk **www.francisfrith.com**